OCEANS ALIVE

Sea Horses

by Ann Herriges

BELLWETHER MEDIA • MINNEAPOLIS, MN

Note to Librarians, Teachers, and Parents:

Blastoff! Readers are carefully developed by literacy experts and combine standards-based content with developmentally appropriate text.

Level 1 provides the most support through repetition of high-frequency words, light text, predictable sentence patterns, and strong visual support.

Level 2 offers early readers a bit more challenge through varied simple sentences, increased text load, and less repetition of high-frequency words.

Level 3 advances early-fluent readers toward fluency through increased text and concept load, less reliance on visuals, longer sentences, and more literary language.

Whichever book is right for your reader, Blastoff! Readers are the perfect books to build confidence and encourage a love of reading that will last a lifetime!

This edition first published in 2007 by Bellwether Media.

No part of this publication may be reproduced in whole or in part without written permission of the publisher. For information regarding permission, write to Bellwether Media Inc., Attention: Permissions Department, Post Office Box 1C, Minnetonka, MN 55345-9998.

Library of Congress Cataloging-in-Publication Data
Herriges, Ann.
  Sea horses / By Ann Herriges.
      p. cm. — (Blastoff! readers) (Oceans alive!)
Summary: "Simple text and supportive images introduce beginning readers to sea horses. Intended for students in kindergarten through third grade."
  Includes bibliographical references and index.
  ISBN-10: 1-60014-020-3 (hardcovers : alk. paper)
  ISBN-13: 978-1-60014-020-4 (hardcovers : alk. paper)
  1. Sea horses—Juvenile literature. I. Title. II. Series.

  QL638.S9H39 2006
  597'.6798–dc22   2006001992

Text copyright © 2007 by Bellwether Media.
Printed in the United States of America.

Table of Contents

The sea horse is a small fish.

The sea horse lives in the
ocean near the shore.

The sea horse's head looks
like a horse's head.

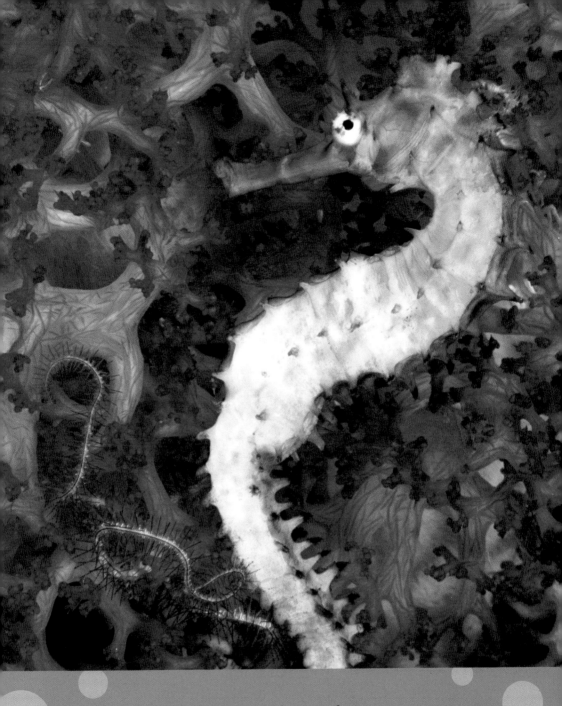

The sea horse has big eyes.
Each eye can look in a
different direction.

gills

The sea horse has **gills**.

Hard **plates** cover the sea horse's body.

fin

The sea horse has a **fin**
on its back.

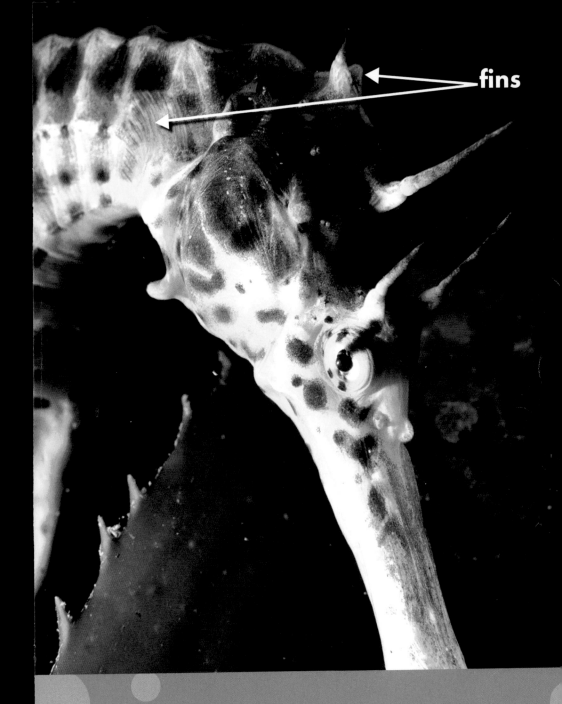

fins

The sea horse has two small fins behind its head.

The sea horse curls its tail
around plants.

This keeps the sea horse
from being carried away
by ocean **currents**.

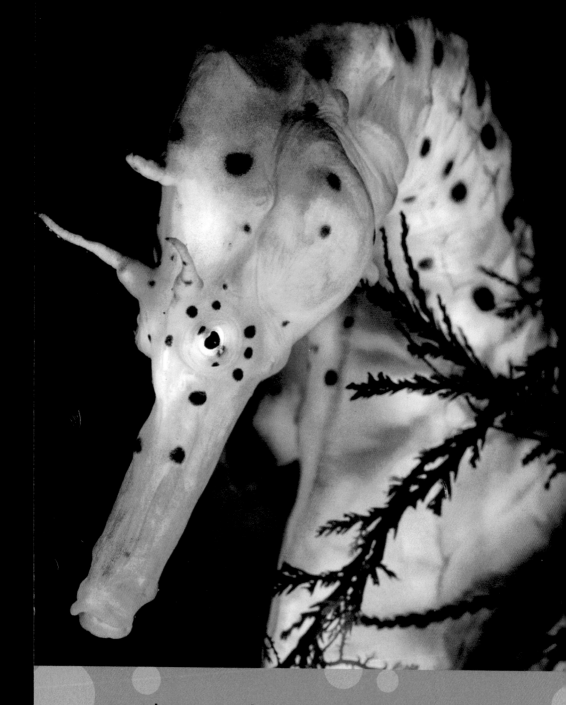

The sea horse has a long **snout** that helps it eat.

The sea horse sucks in tiny
sea animals through its snout.

The sea horse hides from
its enemies.

It changes color to look like its **surroundings**.

pouch

A mother sea horse gives her eggs to the father. He keeps them in a **pouch**.

18

The father sea horse takes
care of the eggs until
they hatch.

Some baby sea horses hold
on to their father after
they hatch.

Then the baby sea horses
swim away into the ocean.

Glossary

current—the movement of water in the ocean

fins—flaps on a fish's body used for moving and steering through the water

gills—slits near the mouth that a fish uses to breathe; the gills move oxygen from the water to the fish's blood.

plates—flat pieces of bony skeleton on the outside of the body; the sea horse's plates are rings that go around the body.

pouch—a flap of skin in which animals carry their young

snout—the long front part of an animal's head that makes up the nose and mouth; the sea horse's snout is a long tube.

surroundings—the area around something; the sea horse can change its color to match the plants, rocks, and coral around it.

To Learn More

AT THE LIBRARY

Andreae, Giles. *Commotion in the Ocean.* Wilton, Conn.: Tiger Tales, 2002.

Carle, Eric. *Mister Seahorse.* New York: Philomel Books, 2004.

Freymann, Saxton. *One Lonely Sea Horse.* New York: Arthur A. Levine Books, 2000.

George, Twig C. *Seahorses.* Brookfield, Conn.: Millbrook Press, 2003.

James, Sylvia M. *Seahorses.* New York: Mondo, 2002.

ON THE WEB

Learning more about sea horses is as easy as 1, 2, 3.

1. Go to www.factsurfer.com

2. Enter "sea horses" into search box.

3. Click the "Surf" button and you will see a list of related web sites.

With factsurfer.com, finding more information is just a click away.

Index

The photographs in this book are reproduced through the courtesy of: Rob Atkins/Getty Images, front cover; Georgette Douwma/Getty Images, pp. 4, 12; Jeff Hunter/Getty Images, p. 5; Jane Burton/Getty Images, p. 6; Michele Westmorland/Getty Images, p. 7; Gail Shumway/Getty Images, p. 8; Juan Martinez, pp. 9, 17; Kim Westerkov/Getty Images, p. 10; Darryl Torckler/Getty Images, p. 11; George Grall/Getty Images, pp. 13, 18-19, 20-21; David Hall/Getty Images, pp. 14, 16; Bill Curtsinger/Getty Images, p. 15.